W9-BYX-943

DESTINATION
THE SUN

GILES SPARROW

PowerKiDS press

New York

NEW HANOVER COUNTY
PUBLIC LIBRARY

New Hanover County Public Library
201 Chestnut Street
Wilmington, North Carolina 28401

Published in 2010 by The Rosen Publishing Group
29 East 21st Street, New York, NY 10010

© 2010 The Brown Reference Group Ltd

All rights reserved. No part of this book may be reproduced in any form
without permission in writing from the publisher, except by a reviewer.

U.S. Editor: Kara Murray

Picture Credits
Key: t – top, b – below, c – center, l – left, r – right. ESA: D. Hardy 27b,
JAXA 10r; John Ballantine: 9l; NASA: GRIN 21, GSFC 10l, 12l, 12c, 12r,
JAXA 8, JHU 23t, JPL 14-15, 17, 29, JPL-Caltech 20-21, MSFC 27t; NASA &
ESA: SOHO TP, 2, 4-5, 9r, 11l, 11c, 11r, 12t, 14, 26; Photos.com: 15, 25l;
Science Photo Library: Chris Butler 28-29, Maximilian Stock Ltd 18l;
Shutterstock: Galyna Andrushko 2-3, 6-7, Cousin_Avi 18-19, Andrea Danti
22-23, Chris Howey 25r, Dmitry Kosterev 7, Roman Krochuk 13, Steven
Newton 24

Front cover: NASA: bl; NASA & ESA: SOHO c; Back cover: NASA & ESA:
SOHO; Backgrounds: NASA

Library of Congress Cataloging-in-Publication Data

Sparrow, Giles.
  Destination the sun / Giles Sparrow. — 1st ed.
      p. cm. — (Destination solar system)
  Includes index.
   ISBN 978-1-4358-3448-4 (lib. bdg.) — ISBN 978-1-4358-3467-5 (pbk.) —
ISBN 978-1-4358-3468-2 (6-pack)
  1. Sun—Juvenile literature. I. Title.
   QB521.5.S752 2010
   523.7—dc22

                                        2009002982

Manufactured in China

CONTENTS

WHERE IS THE SUN?

Earth

The Sun is the nearest star to Earth. It lies at the center of our **solar system**, with all the planets, including Earth, in **orbit** around it.

From Earth, the Sun looks to be almost exactly the same size as the Moon but that is just a coincidence. The Sun is really 400 times wider than the Moon and 400 times farther away from Earth!

SIZE COMPARED TO EARTH
Sun's diameter: 865,000 miles (1,392,000 km)
Earth's diameter: 7,926 miles (12,756 km)

The Sun is at the center of our solar system. It is orbited by the planets and an asteroid belt between Mars and Jupiter.

DISTANCE FROM THE PLANETS

The diagram shows how far the Sun is from the planets that orbit around it. The farthest planets have the longest orbits. The dwarf planet Pluto, for instance, takes 248 years to orbit the Sun.

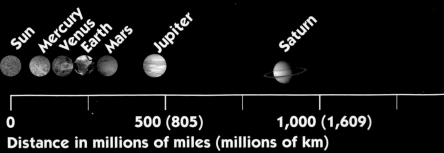

Sun Mercury Venus Earth Mars Jupiter Saturn

0   500 (805)   1,000 (1,609)

Distance in millions of miles (millions of km)

The Sun is vast, nearly 600 times heavier than all the planets put together! Because it is so huge, the Sun's **gravity** is enormous—28 times stronger than Earth's. This force keeps all the planets moving in giant circles around it, called orbits.

Earth lies at an average distance of 93 million miles (150 million km) from the Sun, but the exact distance varies by around 3.1 million miles (5 million km) during the year. The change in distance causes a very slight **temperature** change, but this has nothing to do with the seasons. In fact, Earth is farthest from the Sun when it is summer in the northern hemisphere.

Getting to the Sun

The time it takes to travel from Earth to the Sun depends on how you travel.

By car at 70 miles per hour (113 km/h): 152 years

By rocket at 7 miles per second (11 km/s): 154 days

Time for light and radio signals from the Sun to reach Earth: 8 minutes, 20 seconds

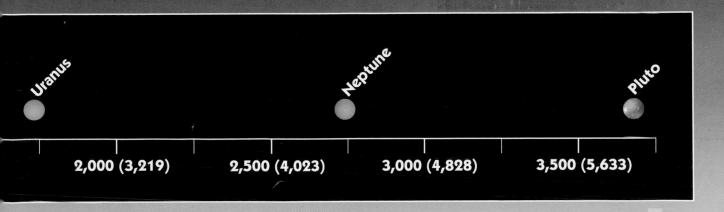

Uranus

Neptune

Pluto

| 2,000 (3,219) | 2,500 (4,023) | 3,000 (4,828) | 3,500 (5,633) |

LOOKING FROM EARTH

Every day, the Sun rises over the eastern horizon, moves across the sky, and sets in the west. People once thought the Sun moved around Earth. However, it only appears to move because Earth is **rotating**.

KEEPING TIME

When measured from the Earth's **equator**, the Sun always rises and sets at the same times each day and follows roughly the same path through the sky.

SEASONS AND THE SUN

Earth's seasons occur because our planet spins on a tilted axis. When the North Pole is pointing toward the Sun, it is bathed in light for longer each day. This makes it summer in the northern half of Earth and winter in the south. When the South Pole is tilted toward the Sun, it is summer in the southern half of Earth and winter in the north.

Earth's seasons are caused by the way parts of the planet point away or toward the Sun at certain times of year.

North Pole

Earth's orbit

South Pole

axis

Sun

summer in northern half of Earth

summer in southern half of Earth

RISE AND SET

In areas north or south of the equator, the Sun's path depends on the time of year, or season. Summers are warmer than winters because the Sun rises higher each day and spends a longer time in the sky.

STAR JOURNEY

Imagine you're about to join a mission to the Sun. Your trip will take several months. Your spaceship has thick shields that can withstand the Sun's strong heat and **radiation**.

At sunrise and sunset, the Sun is shining sideways through a thick layer of air. The air blocks out the blue light, making the sky appear red.

SOLAR ECLIPSE

A solar eclipse happens when the Moon passes in front of the Sun and casts a shadow on Earth. During a total solar eclipse, the Moon hides the Sun's face almost completely, leaving only a faint, outer ring (the corona) in view. The Moon takes about an hour to slowly slide across the Sun and gradually cover it. The period when the Sun is completely blocked out, known as totality, lasts only a few minutes. In that time, the temperature falls, and the sky suddenly darkens, turning day into night! As totality ends, the first rays of sunlight create the diamond ring effect (below).

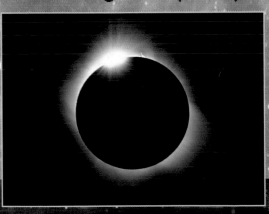

IN ORBIT

After several months, your ship goes into orbit above the Sun. Although the Sun looks like a ball of fire from Earth, your ship's instruments reveal that it is not made of fire but hot, glowing gas.

The corona is the outer layer of the Sun. It is about 8 million miles (13 million km) deep.

HOT LAYER

Even though you are orbiting 1 million miles (1.6 million km) above the Sun's surface, you are still inside its **corona**. The corona is made of the same gas that makes up the Sun, but it is much less **dense**. Sensors on the outside of your spaceship tell you that it is **hydrogen**. However, the Sun's strong heat has torn the **atoms** apart and turned the hydrogen into **plasma**. The plasma in the corona is 1.8 million °F (1 million °C).

SOLAR WIND

Your ship shakes slightly. This is caused by the **solar wind**, a constant stream of plasma that blasts into space from the Sun at up to 2 million miles per hour (3 million km/h). Because of the solar wind, the Sun loses

LIGHT SHIPS

In the future, astronauts might sail through space pushed along by the Sun's light. When light hits a surface, it pushes on it with a tiny force. The spaceships would have huge sails (below) that could harness enough light force to fly through space without using any fuel.

Prominences are thousands of miles (km) long. This one is more than ten times larger than the width of Earth.

Earth

1 million tons (1 million t) of **mass** every second! However, the Sun is so huge—it has a mass of about 2 billion billion billion tons—that it will take a very long time to get smaller!

PLASMA JET

Suddenly, you see a terrifying sight. A jet of yellow plasma has burst out of the Sun, and you are heading straight for it. You prepare yourself—will the spaceship catch fire? But nothing happens. Your spaceship just passes right through the plasma jet.

Your instruments show that the outside temperature has suddenly dropped. The loop of gas was a **prominence**—a cloud of plasma trapped in the Sun's **magnetic field**. Prominences are actually cooler than the corona.

The surface of the Sun is not flat. It is covered in tall, spiky ripples called spicules.

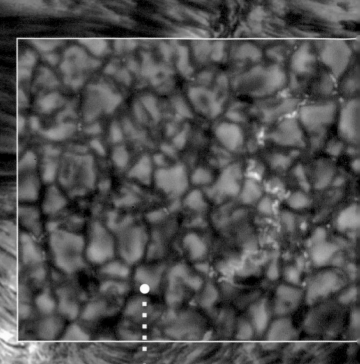

The surface of the Sun has a honeycomb pattern. Each section is about 600 miles (1,000 km) wide.

CLOSER LOOK

The Sun has no solid material in it, so how does it have a surface? You send out a heavily shielded **probe** to find out. As the probe drops through the corona, the temperature rises steadily as the gas gets denser. Then something strange starts to happen. A few thousand miles (km) above the surface, the temperature drops to only a few thousand degrees.

PATTERN SURFACE

The probe's cameras use a filter to block out the blinding light so you get a look at the surface. The surface is seething like a pot of boiling water. It makes a speckled pattern known as **granulation**. The speckles come and go as you watch, but the pattern stays the same. The probe registers the surface temperature as 9,900 °F (5,500 °C).

SEEING THE SUN IN A DIFFERENT LIGHT

Because the Sun is so bright, special filters are used to photograph its surface. Each type of filter reveals different features. Yellow light (below left) shows the Sun's granulation, blue and ultraviolet light (center) shows the bands above and below the equator where sunspots appear, and greener light (right) enhances these bands even more.

UPS AND DOWNS

Something else strange is happening to the surface. Although the probe is falling steadily, the Sun seems to be getting farther away. From your orbit you can see why. Huge areas of the Sun are rising and falling, and the area below the probe is dropping away from it. It is almost as if the Sun were breathing.

You turn the probe's camera to look sideways across the solar surface and you get another surprise. Vast flames seem to be shooting into space. These flames are jets of plasma called **spicules**. Each is about 6,000 miles (10,000 km) tall. That is the distance from Los Angeles to London! Spicules rise up and fall back all in a matter of minutes. Some of the plasma they shoot out of the Sun blows away in the solar wind.

SUNSPOTS AND STORMS

In the glare of the bright surface, you can see dark patches. These are **sunspots**. You send the probe to take a look at them.

SPOTS ON THE SUN

Sunspots occur in clusters near the Sun's equator. As you get close to one, you see that its dark center is surrounded by a slightly lighter area where hairlike rays spread out from the center. The whole spot is huge—big enough to swallow Earth. The temperature of the sunspot is a searing 6,300 °F (3,500 °C), but it looks dark because the surrounding area is even brighter and hotter.

Sunspots appear as dark patches. They are most common near the Sun's equator.

A solar flare bursts out of a sunspot, blasting radiation into space.

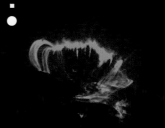

TWISTED FIELDS

Sunspots are formed as the Sun's magnetic field (1) gets twisted. This happens because the equator spins faster than the poles (2). Sunspots form where the field loops in and out of the surface (3). The field slowly gets worse over a number of years creating more and more sunspots and solar storms (4).

MAGNETIC LOOPS

Your ship's magnetic sensors are now showing very high readings. This is because a powerful **magnetic field** is coming out of the sunspot, just like Earth's magnetic field comes out from the **poles**. Is the sunspot a magnetic pole? Poles come in pairs, so where is the other end of this magnetic field? You fly the probe along the direction of the field. It loops high into the corona before sinking down over another nearby sunspot.

BLAST FROM BELOW

Suddenly your magnetic sensors go haywire, the field between the sunspots is shifting. You move your ship away from the area and watch to see what happens. As the magnetic field rearranges itself, it heats up the base of the corona. Then, with a blinding flash, a jet of plasma shoots out from above the sunspots and bursts past you through the corona as a **solar flare**. The ship's detectors record bursts of **ultraviolet light** and **X-rays**, as well as bright visible light.

(1)

(2)

field lines

(3)

(4)

sunspot

When solar flares reach Earth, they produce shimmering lights, or auroras, near Earth's poles.

This set of pictures shows the activity of the Sun between 1996 and 2006.

2001, high activity

SOLAR CYCLE

The number of sunspots, prominences, and solar flares produced by the Sun changes from year to year. The changes follow an 11-year solar cycle. The activity increases in the first few years as the Sun's magnetic field gets more twisted. Then the activity settles down again because the magnetic field is so twisted that its curls and loops begin to cancel each other out. As a result, sunspots become less common.

WARNING!

You have arrived at the height of the Sun's activity. After the narrow escape with the solar flare, you decide to move out to a safer distance. You are just in time, since a warning siren tells you that your spaceship has detected dangerous radiation. You cannot see where it is coming from at first. Then you use a filter to block out the bright light. What you see next makes you gasp.

GIANT STORM

An enormous bubble has formed over a cluster of sunspots and is rising from the corona, growing to an unbelievable size. Your instruments show that it has billions of tons (t) of plasma in it. The giant bubble is a Sun storm, or **coronal mass ejection**. This storm is not heading for you but it is heading straight for Earth! Luckily our planet is protected from the plasma by its own magnetic field.

Coronal mass ejections can be as large as the Sun itself.

When astronomers studied sunspot records during the 1800s, they made a strange discovery. Between 1645 and 1715, there were almost no sunspots. It was as if the solar cycle had stopped.

This period may be linked to very cold weather on Earth, a period known as the Little Ice Age. Many rivers froze over during this time. The Thames River in London, England, often froze so thick that people held "frost fairs" on the ice (below). The Thames River has rarely frozen since.

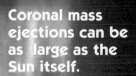

INSIDE THE SUN

Using what you learned on your mission, you can now start to piece together a complete picture of the Sun.

GAS BALL

Like most stars, the Sun is made of hydrogen. The second-most-common **element** is **helium**.

If you could split the Sun open, you would see that it has three zones: the **core**, the **radiative zone**, and the **convective zone**.

SLOW PROGRESS

All the Sun's energy is generated in the core, which takes up about a quarter of the Sun's width. This energy forces its way out of the Sun as light and other forms of radiation. However, the plasma in the radiative zone is so tightly packed that the radiation cannot move through it easily. Light rays keep colliding with particles of

The Sun's core is an amazing 27 million °F (15 million °C). Energy from the core takes 100,000 years to pass through the radiative zone, ten days to travel through the convective zones, and then just eight minutes to reach Earth.

The colors of the light coming from the Sun tell us what elements are in the corona. Two common ones are sodium and calcium.

corona

photosphere

convective zone

radiative zone

core

plasma and are taken in and then let out again in different directions. All this back and forth means that the radiation takes more than 100,000 years to work its way out through the radiative zone, steadily losing energy as it goes.

SHINING THROUGH

The top of the radiative zone traps all the light coming up from below and heats up rapidly. When gases heat up, they rise—a process called convection. The hot plasma bubbles up through the convective zone until it reaches the Sun's surface, the **photosphere**. The photosphere is see-through, so light and heat shines through it and out into space. When the plasma has let out its energy as sunlight, it cools down and sinks back to take in more energy from below.

HOW THE SUN SHINES

The Sun is the only source of light in the solar system. It makes it using a process called **nuclear fusion**.

The Sun's heat powers Earth's wind and drives this turbine.

This man is inside a fusion reactor, which re-creates the conditions in the Sun's core. Someday reactors like this might make our electricity.

SQUEEZED INSIDE

The Sun has enormous gravity. As a result, the plasma in the core is squeezed into a very tight space, making it denser and hotter. The heat and **pressure** start nuclear fusion.

INSIDE ATOMS

A hydrogen atom usually has two parts: a **proton** forms the center, or **nucleus**, of the atom. A small particle called an **electron** moves around the proton. In the Sun the atoms are split apart as plasma.

There are three stages of fusion: 1) Two protons collide. One of them lets out radiation and a tiny particle called a neutrino. That proton is now a neutron. 2) The proton-neutron pair fuses with another proton. This lets out more energy and forms a triple particle. 3) Two triple particles fuse to form a helium nucleus, letting out heat and light.

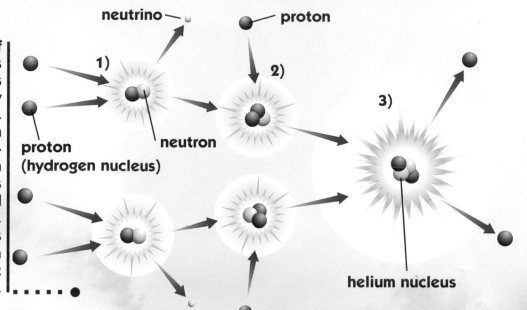

neutrino

proton

1)

2)

3)

proton
(hydrogen nucleus)

neutron

helium nucleus

EINSTEIN'S EQUATION

Albert Einstein's famous equation $E = mc^2$ explains why nuclear fusion lets out so much energy. When protons fuse together in the Sun, a tiny bit of their mass is converted into energy. According to the equation, the energy (E) equals the mass (m) times the speed of light squared (c^2). The speed of light squared is a huge number, 9 followed by 16 zeros! So even a small amount of mass can turn into a vast quantity of energy. Every second, the Sun turns about four million tons (t) of its mass into pure energy!

ENERGY SOURCE

In the Sun's core, protons are pushed into each other. Protons are positively charged and they normally **repel** each other. However, protons in the core collide with such force that they fuse, or join together. This is nuclear fusion. It lets out vast amounts of energy and turns hydrogen into helium.

Sunlight is the source of energy for Earth's plants.

HOW THE SUN FORMED

The Sun is one of 200 billion stars that make up the Milky Way **galaxy**. Stars are always dying and forming throughout the galaxy, recycling the same material over and over.

STAR CREATION

The material in the Sun and planets was formed billions of years ago, when a huge star blew itself apart in an enormous explosion called a **supernova**. This explosion created all the atoms in the solar system, including those in our bodies.

Supernovas happen when very large stars run out of fuel. The star crushes itself in seconds, and this causes a blast wave that shoots the star's atoms into space.

The Sun and the rest of the solar system formed from a disk of dust and gas about 4.5 billion years ago.

RIPPLED CLOUD

The dead star becomes a huge cloud of gas and dust called a **nebula**. A passing star can send a shock wave rippling through a nebula causing parts of the cloud to become denser. These squeezed areas have just enough gravity to start getting smaller and pulling more material in. This is the process that gave birth to our Sun.

AND THERE WAS LIGHT

The gas and dust cloud began to spin, becoming a disk, with most of the matter in a collapsing ball of gas at its center. Inside the ball of gas, the atoms collided and started to heat up, creating a dim glow. The pressure and temperature inside grew higher until nuclear fusion could begin. Fusion spread through the core in an instant, and the Sun lit up as if someone had flipped a switch!

Stars are forming inside this nebula, called the Pillars of Hercules.

THE SUN'S FAMILY

The newly formed Sun was surrounded by a disk of gas, ice, and dust. Over millions of years, these materials began to form into planets, moons, and **asteroids**.

ORBITING COMPANIONS

Today we know of eight planets orbiting the Sun. The closest are small worlds made of rock and metal: Mercury, Venus, Earth, and Mars. Beyond Mars is the asteroid belt, a cloud of rubble left over after the planets had formed. Way beyond this lie the giant planets: enormous Jupiter, Saturn and its

Mercury
Venus
Earth
Mars

magnificent rings, Uranus, and Neptune. Unlike the inner planets, these are huge worlds made of gas and ice. Farther out are dozens of icy dwarf planets. So far only two of these distant dwarf planets have been named: Pluto and Eris.

Jupiter

ROCKY WORLDS

Different types of planets formed because of their distance from the Sun. Close to the Sun, the solar wind soon blew away gases such as hydrogen and helium, leaving behind water, gas, dust, and glassy particles. These materials formed the solid, inner planets. Another solid world would have formed in the asteroid belt, but Jupiter's enormous gravity prevented the rocks from clumping together.

Dwarf planets orbit far from the Sun in a region known as the Kuiper Belt.

Saturn

Pluto

Neptune

Uranus

This composite photograph shows the planets that make up the solar system. The order and sizes are correct but the distance between each planet is not.

COLD AS ICE

The outer planets formed from a mixture of hydrogen, helium, and ice. Jupiter and Saturn formed quickly, pulling in vast amounts of gas. Uranus and Neptune formed more slowly. Most of the hydrogen and helium around them blew away before they could capture it, so these planets are mainly ice. Pluto and Eris formed from ice debris at the edge of the solar system.

STUDYING THE SUN

In ancient times, people worshipped the Sun as a source of light and heat. They also followed it through the sky as a guide to the seasons.

GOD IN THE SKY

The ancient Egyptians had not one but four Sun gods: Aten (the disk of the Sun), Kephri (the rising Sun), Ra (the midday Sun), and Atum (the setting Sun). The ancient Greeks' Sun god was called Helios. He drove the Sun across the sky in a chariot every day.

Scientists studying the light from the Sun discovered it could be split into a spectrum of colors.

The Romans held big winter celebrations on the shortest day of the year, when the Sun is up for just a few hours, to celebrate the rebirth of the Sun. Christians celebrate Christmas around the same time.

AT THE CENTER

The first **astronomers** believed that Earth was at the center of the universe, with the Sun, Moon, and planets circling it. The Greek scientist Aristarchus knew that the Sun was much bigger and farther away than the Moon. He was the first to suggest that the Sun stands still and Earth and the other planets move around it, but his ideas were forgotten.

Centuries later, in 1543, Polish priest Nicolaus Copernicus published a book about how the solar system orbited the Sun. In the early 1600s, the invention of the telescope allowed astronomers to see that that is exactly what it does.

TEMPLES OF THE SUN

The ancient people of America were Sun worshippers. Before European settlers arrived about 500 years ago, Mayans, Toltecs, Aztecs, and Incas all built temples that lined up with the rising and setting Sun at important times of the year. The Aztecs even made human sacrifices during eclipses to make sure the Sun returned. An Incan celebration (below) honoring the Sun god is still practiced in Peru today.

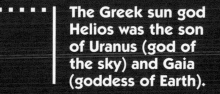

The Greek sun god Helios was the son of Uranus (god of the sky) and Gaia (goddess of Earth).

BLINDING LIGHT

You cannot look at the Sun through a telescope. The bright light would burn your eyes and make you blind. Instead, early astronomers projected images of the Sun onto a screen. They could see sunspots and prominences, which showed that the Sun was more than just a glowing orb.

ROBOT EXPLORERS

Space probes have changed our understanding of the Sun. Probes can look at the star more clearly since they are outside of Earth's atmosphere. They also look at different **wavelengths** of radiation, including invisible ultraviolet light and X-rays.

One of the most successful missions was *Ulysses*, a European probe sent off in 1990. Its orbit takes it high over the Sun's north and south poles, far above and below the rest of the solar system. *Ulysses* discovered large holes in the corona over the poles.

The *Solar and Heliospheric Observatory* (*SOHO*) was a Sun probe sent into space in 1995 by American and European scientists.

The *Hinode* probe orbits Earth directly over the sunset line that moves around the planet. It can see the Sun 24 hours a day.

LOOKING AT LIGHT

The *Solar and Heliospheric Observatory*, or *SOHO*, orbits the Sun about 900,000 miles (1.5 million km) from Earth. *SOHO* is made to look at the Sun's corona using ultraviolet telescopes and also to measure the rise and fall of the Sun's surface as sunquakes ripple through it.

The *Transition Region and Coronal Explorer*, or *TRACE*, was sent into space by **NASA** in 1998 to study the corona, especially the region at the base where the temperature rises well above that of the photosphere.

Ulysses had a four-year journey to the Sun. It traveled via Jupiter to get into the correct orbit.

27

THE END OF THE SUN

About five billion years in the future, the Sun will run out of hydrogen fuel and die. What will happen to Earth and the rest of the solar system?

GROWING OLD

Astronomers know a lot about the life of stars because there are so many stars to study. Big stars die with a huge explosion called a supernova, but small stars like the Sun die in a less violent way.

As the Sun's hydrogen gets used up, the core spread outs, and the Sun will swell to about 100 times wider,

A red giant Sun will blast away Earth's air and ocean, turning the planet into a lifeless rock.

The Crab Nebula was formed when a star exploded in 1054. •••••

becoming a type of star called a **red giant.** The red giant will swallow the planets Mercury and Venus. Earth will become the first planet.

FINAL PHASE

The giant Sun's fusion will be fueled by helium not hydrogen. The Sun will get smaller as the helium runs out, and the Sun will swell up again. This time there is no way back. The Sun will keep swelling, blowing away its outer layers to form a gas cloud called a planetary nebula. At the heart of the nebula, the Sun's core will turn into a tiny star called a **white dwarf** about the size of Earth. A white dwarf is very dense.

GOOD-BYE EARTH

The Sun's death will mean the end of life on Earth. If humans are still around, they will not be living in the solar system. Perhaps we will then have the technology needed to make homes across the galaxy.

GLOSSARY

asteroids (AS-teh-roydz) Large chunks of rock left over from when the planets formed.

astronomers (uh-STRAH-nuh-merz) Scientists who study planets and other objects in space.

atom (A-temz) Tiny particles of matter.

convective zone (kon-VEK-tiv ZOHN) The region below the Sun's surface where hot plasma bubbles up to the surface, letting out light before sinking back down.

core (KOR) The central part of a star.

corona (kuh-ROH-nah) The outer layer of the Sun.

coronal mass ejection (KOR-uh-nul MAS ih-JEK-shun) An eruption of a huge amount of plasma from the Sun's corona.

dense (DENTS) Having a lot of weight squeezed into a space.

electron (ih-LEK-tron) A negatively charged particle in the outer part of an atom.

element (EH-luh-ment) A chemical that cannot be split into any other chemicals.

equator (ih-KWAY-tur) The imaginary line around the center of a planet, moon, or star that is located midway between the poles.

galaxy (GA-lik-see) A collection of millions of stars held together by gravity.

granulation (gran-yuh-LAY-shun) A speckled pattern of dark lines around brighter areas on the Sun's surface.

gravity (GRA-vih-tee) The force that pulls objects together. The heavier or closer an object is, the stronger its gravity.

helium (HEE-lee-um) The second-most-common element in the universe.

hydrogen (HY-dreh-jen) The simplest, lightest, and most common element in the universe.

magnetic field (mag-NEH-tik FEELD) A region of space around a planet, moon, or star where a compass can detect the North Pole.

mass (MAS) The measure of the amount of material in an object.

NASA (NA-suh) The National Aeronautics and Space Administration, the U.S. space agency in charge of sending people and probes into space.

nebula (NEH-byuh-luh) A huge cloud of gas and dust in space.

nuclear fusion (NOO-klee-ur FYOO-zhun) The process in which atoms fuse together, letting out vast amounts of energy.

nucleus (NOO-klee-us) The center of an atom.

orbit (OR-bit) A movement around a heavier, and usually larger, object caused by the effect of the heavier object's gravity.

photosphere (FOH-toh-sfeer) The surface of the Sun.

plasma (PLAZ-muh) A gas so hot that its atoms are torn apart into smaller particles.

poles (POHLZ) The top or bottom ends of the axis of a planet, moon, or star.

pressure (PREH-shur) A force that pushes on something.

probe (PROHB) A robot spaceship sent to study the solar system.

prominence (PRAH-mih-nens) A giant arch of plasma that forms over the Sun's surface.

proton (PROH-ton) A positively charged particle in the nucleus of an atom.

radiation (ray-dee-AY-shun) Energy let out in rays from a source. Heat and light are types of radiation.

radiative zone (RAY-dee-ay-tiv ZOHN) The region surrounding the Sun's core.

red giant (RED JY-unt) An old star that has swollen with age and turned red.

repel (rih-PEL) To push against.

rotating (ROH-tayt-ing) Spinning around a central point, or axis.

solar flare (SOH-ler FLAYR) A sudden burst of plasma and radiation from a sunspot at the bottom of the corona.

solar system (SOH-ler SIS-tem) The planets, asteroids, and comets that orbit the Sun.

solar wind (SOH-ler WIND) The constant stream of plasma that travels out of the Sun.

spicules (SPIK-yoolz) Short-lived jets of plasma that shoot out of the Sun's surface.

sunspots (SUN-spots) Dark, cool regions on the Sun's surface.

supernova (soo-per-NOH-vuh) A colossal explosion produced by the death of a large star.

temperature (TEM-pur-cher) How hot something is.

ultraviolet light (ul-truh-VY-uh-let LYT) A type of invisible light given off by high-energy objects.

wavelengths (WAYV-lengths) Properties of radiation. We see light of different wavelengths as different colors and light of mixed wavelengths as white.

white dwarf (HWYT DWAWRF) A dim star about the same size as Earth but much denser.

X-rays (EKS-rayz) Invisible radiation that is stronger than ultraviolet light and given off by very hot objects.

INDEX

WEB SITES

Due to the changing nature of Internet links, PowerKids Press has developed an online list of Web sites related to the subject of this book. This site is updated regularly. Please use this link to access the list:
www.powerkidslinks.com/dsol/sun/

DISCARDED

ML   12/09